Haunted Newport
by Eleyne Austen Sharp

*"I do believe in spooks. I do believe in spooks.
I do—I do—I do—I do—I DO believe in spooks!"*

(The Cowardly Lion in The Wizard of Oz)

OP EN  M IND

The stories presented in this book are based on legend
and actual testimonials.

Every reasonable attempt has been made by the author to prevent
inaccuracies. For reasons of privacy, the identities and addresses
of some eyewitnesses have been withheld at their request.

Published by austen sharp
P.O. Box 12
Newport, RI 02840

copyright © 1999 by Eleyne Austen Sharp

Cover art by Melissa Martin Ellis

ISBN 0-9652589-2-0

Printed in the U.S.A.
First printing, September 1999

Information on pages 57 and 58 courtesy of Newport County Convention and Visitors
Bureau.

Photos on pages 6, 11, 26, 43, 46, 51, 56 and 71 courtesy of Melissa Martin Ellis

Haunted Newport™ logo is a trademark of austen sharp

ACKNOWLEDGEMENTS

This book would not have been possible without the contributions of many people.

My sincere appreciation to Kristin Adamo, Richard Alexander, Winthrop Baker, Ted Beaumont, Jane Berriman, Dennis Blair, Bogart Blakeley, Mrs. G. Bogart Blakeley, Susan Burns, Margaretta Clulow, Sonja Colabella, Betty Conklin, Melissa Cordone, Kathleen Marie Crawford, Amy Croke, Grant Edmondson, Randy Fabricant, Selma Fabricant, Kathryn Farrington, Tom Gannon, Frank S. Hale, Jade Hall, Keith Henry, Joya Hoyt, Dan Keating, Tanya Kelley, Patrick Kirby, Lindsey Kusic, Laura LaDuke, Vicki Little, Dr. Sarah Littlefield, Virginia Long, Tylor Marking, Rafael Medina, Newport Public Library, Stephan Nicolas, Anthony Nicolosi, Leonard Panaggio, Martine Putier, Maxime Putier, Anita Rafael, Benjamin Reed, Jr., Rob Reimer, Chris Rondina, Dr. Virginia Ross, Mary Samuels, Deidre Sharp, Margaret Small, Virginia Smith, Patricia Cahill Taft, Donald Tinney, Harle Tinney, Ruth Tinney, Constance Trewblood and Ed Warren.

For her beautiful cover, good humor and great wisdom, I thank Newport artist Melissa Martin Ellis.

Finally, a very special thanks to my husband, Nick, for his love, encouragement and *extreme* patience. It's not easy living with ghosts, you know. (Of course, you should hear what the ghosts are saying about us!)

—Eleyne Austen Sharp

Haunted Newport

That Creepy Feeling

You are alone and uneasy about it. A shadow darts across the walls and up the stairs, but it's not your shadow. The windows rattle with the blow of a Nor'easter yet there is no wind. The floorboards are creaking and your heart thumps loudly, but it cannot drown out the eerie, hollow whispering of a stranger's voice. Surely, you are imagining things. No, there is something here. The idea that your every move is being watched sends tiny electric shivers throughout your body. If you weren't such a practical person, you would swear the place was haunted. But you don't believe in ghosts—or do you?

Since the beginning of our existence, we mortals have been fascinated with death and the hereafter. And even if we never spy a true phantom in our lifetime, chances are we have either read about spooks (*MacBeth, A Christmas Carol, The Bible*) or seen their likenesses on television or at the movies ("Topper", "The Ghost and Mrs. Muir", "Casper", "Ghostbusters"). Whether they appear slimy, cute, or utterly charming, ghosts are nothing to be afraid of, the experts tell us. They are merely dead people with unfinished business.

* * *

Virginia Smith conducts a popular ghost tour at Belcourt Castle and likes to talk about ghosts so much that you could call them her passion. She is writing a book on hauntings in Europe and the United States and, since moving to Newport, Rhode Island, has discovered over sixty haunted houses.

Her first eerie encounter occurred when she was nine years old. While sitting at the piano in her grandmother's music room, Virginia watched, transfixed, as the bodies of a man and woman materialized before her. "They were visible only from the waist up and appeared to be having a tremendous argument."

Virginia could hear sounds emanating from their lips but was unable to understand their words, a peculiarity of what she calls *whisper ghosts*. "It sounds like the English language is being used, but you cannot make sense of what they're saying."

After running home to her mother and describing what she had seen, Virginia was shown an early photograph of her grandmother. The pretty young woman was one of the ghosts, alright, but how could that be? Virginia's grandmother was very much alive!

Then her mother revealed a secret about the "stalker", the smitten young man her happily married grandmother was forced to deal with many years before. Today, Virginia suspects that the angry male ghost in her grandmother's music room was the stalker, and the scene she had witnessed was actually recreated by the intense, negative energy of long ago. While she isn't sure why some spirits appear solid and others are filmy, Virginia is certain that one could walk right by a ghost and not know it.

"Of course," she says, "the giveaway is when they're walking a few feet off the ground!"

Just like cats that go straight to the one person in the room who doesn't like them, spirits seem to latch onto Virginia like barnacles.

"I'm still afraid of ghosts. It's distressing when anyone has a confrontation with something that is simply non-explicable in every logical term. You want to find a logical explanation."

Logical or not, Virginia cannot deny her fascination with the supernatural and, for the sake of her book, investigates places which are reputed to be haunted. "I have sensed and seen them, heard them and smelled them."

So what does a real ghost smell like? "It's unmistakable," she says. "It's a combination of violets and rot and burned out electric fuses."

***

Jade Hall doesn't generally smell ghosts, but she certainly knows when she finds one, because "the hairs on my arm stand up."

A native Virginian, Jade balks at calling herself a psychic, even though she has had intuitive experiences most of her life.

"I don't like the label 'psychic'," she explains, "because people are intimidated by those who are able to predict the future. To see what they really are—people are scared of that."

As a child, Jade read tarot cards for her friends, a bit surprising when you consider that she had never even read a book about the subject. Yet instinctively she knew what each colorful, detailed card represented.

It was nearly three a.m. one morning when young Jade awoke to what felt like someone shaking her leg. No human was present but Jade's body was bathed in a strange white light and she wondered why she felt so cold. Frightened, the little girl ran to the bathroom but, to her horror, the light had followed her and was relentless in its pursuit. Back in her bedroom, she was greeted by the milky figure of a ghost woman. The next day, Jade and her sisters exchanged nearly identical stories—each one of them had been visited by the persistent spirit!

Christopher Rondina is another person who is one hundred percent certain that ghosts exist. Since his first ghost experience in Newport in 1982, the Middletown author of *Vampire Legends of Rhode Island* is often sought after to investigate homes in Newport County.

"I wouldn't give myself much credit as a psychic," Chris says, "but I have a pretty good logical understanding of what hauntings are. And I'm good at calming people's fears."

These fears, he says, stem from people's impressions after viewing movies like "Poltergeist" and "Ghostbusters", which he doubts bear much resemblance to actuality.

"We tend to have an image of ghosts that is created by the cinema, that ghosts can come out, have a conversation, throw some plates across the room and cause things to light on fire."

One of his most memorable run-ins was the evening he attended a friend's birthday party and spent a lot of time playing a Ouija board. Afterwards, when he had returned home and gone to bed, an apparition of light appeared.

"I didn't believe that it was real, I thought it was a hallucination." Even so, Chris rose from his bed in a dream-like state and walked boldly through the space where the light shone.

"I immediately collapsed on the other side. I felt exceptionally cold, like I had walked through a vacuum in space." Then he began to sob.

Sleeping in the same room was a friend, who suddenly sat upright: "I'm so sorry," the friend announced. "I never meant to hurt you. You never let me grow up. I loved you so much, but you never let me grow up."

Later, when he and his pal discussed the event at length, Chris determined that whatever it was that had made him feel such incredible sorrow had somehow transferred to his friend, perhaps a more viable medium for its message.

***

For *Susan Burns,* psychic experiences are the norm, not the exception. When she was 7 years old, Susan saw the figure of a boy she knew standing in her family's basement. The next day at school, she

Island Cemetery

heard a tragic story. The boy had hung himself!

Once, while walking past Thompson Middle School on Broadway, Susan heard the busy sounds of construction. Turning to look, she witnessed what she believes was a psychic re-enactment of the school being built many years before.

"There has not been a house I've lived in, in Newport—whether it be the Point section, around Newport Hospital or the Broadway area," says Susan, "where I haven't seen, felt or smelled a ghost in one form or another."

She recalls the night she was startled by one particularly frightening ghost in her apartment near Newport Hospital. The dark-clothed phantom was riding a black steed when he appeared in Susan's bedroom, reeking of lilacs.

"I felt like this energy was actually trying to smother me," she says.   So she said the *Lord's Prayer* and instantly returned to "a place of safety."

With these kinds of experiences, one is surprised to learn Susan's advice is to be unafraid of ghosts. "In a very small percentage of cases, there are energies that are very unfriendly," she explains. "But no matter how you look at this, we are the masters of our own space and reality. And we are the ones that have the right of way."

***

Is your resident ghost subject to temper tantrums? Do cups and saucers fly overhead at the slightest provocation? Are you frequently tripped and shoved or even brutalized?   When things get bad, folks call on *Ed and Lorraine Warren*.

Call them "ghostbusters" or "ghost hunters"—they don't mind. For over 40 years, this busy Connecticut couple have investigated hauntings from North America to Australia, including the famous "Amityville Horror House" on Long Island.

One of their Newport County cases involved a millionaire whose death in the 1940s was accepted as suicide. The man had lived with his wife and sister-in-law, and his spirit had been seen wandering his waterfront mansion.

Years later, residents found the shell of an old bullet , determining that the millionaire had not committed suicide after all. He was murdered by his sister-in-law, Ed says, and his spirit continues to haunt the mansion to this day. "He was killed very suddenly. He's so confused that he doesn't even know that he's dead."

Have you ever come home from an auction or yard sale, convinced that you have just purchased the most wonderful antique ever? How would you feel if you knew an uninvited guest had hitched a ride aboard your Queen Anne chair? Ed believes that spirits are able to project their energy into objects quite easily, and items found at flea markets or antique shops are suspect.

Such was the case of one Newport woman. "She was given an antique mirror—quite big—probably about six feet high. All of a sudden, her two children started to see things in the mirror. First there were flashes of light. And then they saw a man looking out at them. Then the mother started seeing it and then they had its infestation in the house."

Seven out of every ten cases investigated by The Warren's New England Society for Psychic Research are the result of using a Ouija board. In one extraordinary example, a 54-year old woman had had eighteen exorcisms.

Says Ed: "I've seen the hair torn out of her head, I've seen bites appear on her body. I've felt her being punched by blows."

***

Could your own house be haunted? Well, there may be a ghost of a chance. The older a house is, the more there is an opportunity of a tragedy to create the ghost syndrome.

Chris Rondina says that some hauntings involve a spirit repeating an action that occurred during their life, or a replay of the moment of their death. These ghosts are generally not interactive and the spirits that do speak to people usually have a limited vocabulary, as well as one burning issue that was never resolved.

"They're more like a movie on a constant loop, playing themselves out over and over again. They are incapable of breaking their pattern, because they're not really a presence at all."

If you think your newly-built home makes you automatically exempt from hauntings, don't celebrate quite yet.

Says Susan Burns: "If the land has been walked on by many people or if it was a roadway at one time or the house was built over a place of great activity, very often in new houses this energy will come in."

So how do you get rid of them? Try the no-nonsense approach. Talk directly to the ghost and remind it that it is dead, after all, and needs to stop hanging around you and go towards the Light of God.

Sprinkling salt, striking gongs and lighting white candles may help, or you might try slamming a door several times in succession. Experts say the ghost will get caught between the door and the frame and will grow tired of the torture and leave.

Virginia Smith prefers a gentler approach. "I'd say, 'I'm delighted to share the house with you, but I'd like to set some ground rules'." She would ask the specter not to enter her bedroom at night, but to let her know if she was in danger of fire or theft.

"Being psychic, people have asked me to come into their homes because they have felt something or seen something," says Susan Burns. "In some cases, I've been asked to remove this energy from their environment. For me, this is done with a lot of love, a lot of integrity and a lot of prayer."

When asked about seances, Susan exclaims, "I think they are fantastic...an absolutely terrific medium for people that are like-minded to join together and put their collective energy together to actually open a doorway to communicate with the other world."

Maybe a ghost can't hurt you, but it could make you hurt yourself, as Jade Hall believes. Still, if you happen to have a strong belief in God, you are especially protected.

But what if you're *not* a religious person?

Ed Warren laughs. "Just like there are no atheists in foxholes, there are no atheists in haunted houses."

Legend and Lore

What would you do if you ran into the famous Benjamin Franklin? Would you discuss politics? Electricity? The chain of craft stores which bear his name?

When the now defunct Franklin Printing was located on Thames Street, some 20th century employees swore they could hear and see the ghost of the inventive patriot. Surprising? Not when you consider that it was Ben's brother, James, who founded the shop in 1727.

Around Halloween time, when thoughts are turned to bright full moons and headless hobgoblins, a group of folks get together at the White Horse Tavern to exchange tales of the supernatural. They are indeed a brave lot since the tavern, itself, is said to be haunted.

***

One of the stories *Anita Rafael* likes to tell is about a 17th century trial in which the defendant was found guilty and hanged—condemned by the testimony of a ghost!

"It was in 1673 when old Mrs. Cornell of Newport was found burned to death. This was not so suspicious because women were often burned to death by their cooking fires. As a precaution, some women would wear wool aprons and clothing because if the wool caught a spark, it would only smolder, not go up in flames. So it was strange that Mrs. Cornell was wearing wool clothing at the time of her death.

The other peculiar thing about this incident was that at the time Mrs. Cornell would have been burning to death, nobody reported smelling smoke nor heard her scream or cry. It seemed a bit suspicious and there was an investigation, but it was determined that she had indeed died an accidental death by fire.

A few days later, a Quaker named Mr. Briggs went to City Hall and proclaimed to the magistrate that Mrs. Cornell had not burned to death after all. 'Last night, as I laid in my bed, the ghost of my dear sister came to me and woke me up and told me exactly how she had been murdered.' By Briggs' account, the ghost had lifted up her clothes and showed him the wounds that had caused her death.

The magistrate ordered a team of surgeons to Mrs. Cornell's grave and conducted an autopsy. They found much clotted blood about the body cavity and when they had scraped away the burnt tissue on her chest, they indeed found a stab wound made by a sharp object.

The ghost had also related that it was her son, Thomas, who had committed the murder with a piece from her spinning wheel. Witnesses corroborated that they had heard Thomas and his mother arguing earlier in the day. Thomas was arrested and Briggs gave Mrs. Cornell's testimony at the trial.

Facing overwhelming evidence, Thomas was sentenced to hang, although he proclaimed his innocence throughout. His pleas to be buried next to his mother went ignored."

***

Legend also has it that a specter was seen at the historic **John Banister House** on Pelham Street. Built in 1751, the gambrel-roofed house was used as British General William Prescott's headquarters during the Revolutionary War. Centuries later, a guest complained of being awakened by a "man" in 19th century dress. The ghost was singing her a love ballad!

***

As haunted houses go, **Cozzens House** was fairly notorious. Located in The Point section at the corner of Warner and Farewell Streets, it is one of the country's first double structures, built in the late 1700s by two brothers, William and Joseph Cozzens. Supposedly, a family was murdered in the house and afterwards, the victims' faces would appear on the finials of the fence posts. This story got quite a bit of press in the 1800s and it is unfortunate that the haunted fence was replaced and destroyed.

***

A ghost in an 18th century naval uniform was seen on several occasions at **La Petite Auberge**, the elegant French restaurant located at Washington Square. Thought to be Stephen Decatur, Sr. (the privateersman who was born in the small colonial house), the phantom first debuted in 1976. He has been described as a grey-haired gentleman wearing a maroon, double-breasted military-type shirt.

***

The house lights were up at the **Casino Theater** when one local director thought he detected three images sitting in the balcony. When they suddenly vanished, the director quipped to his friend that the ghostly trio were most likely the theater's amorous architect, Stanford White—accompanied by his wife and mistress!

Beautifully eerie is **Purgatory Chasm**, the 160-foot long cliff which overlooks Second Beach in Middletown. According to legend, there was once an Indian squaw who was accused of murdering a white man. As punishment, Hobomoko (aka the Indian Satan) seized the squaw and took her to the cliff, chopped off her head and threw the remains of her body into the chasm.

The squaw's restless spirit is said to haunt the area, although it is unknown whether she walks the earth with head or without.

***

The tale of **The Sea Bird** is one that continues to intrigue and baffle. Following a violent storm in 1750, this mysterious brigantine sailed into Newport Harbor and was found deserted, except for a dog and a cat.

Had the crew been murdered?   Or did they drown?   And why was the stove still warm, the captain's table set, and a fire burning brightly in the galley?

Since remains of the crew were never found, some question whether *The Sea Bird* was empty after all.   Could it be the spirits of the dead sailors themselves who continued to keep the two-masted schooner "ship-shape?"

***

On **Sunnyside Place**, there is a house where everyone who rented it moved out in a few weeks. The story goes that there were two young girls who had died of tuberculosis on the third floor of the house. Not only do the girls' spirits haunt the building, but people claim that everyone who has lived there since has acquired psychological problems.

***

Have you ever wondered why it is so difficult to get good help these days? During the early 1900's, there was a maid cleaning a mansion on the corner of Bellevue and Narragansett. Alas, her end of the season cleaning came to an abrupt halt when she found herself trapped in an elevator.   No one ever heard her cries and the poor woman's body wasn't found until the following spring. Witnesses say her spirit has been seen in the vicinity.

***

Inside his former home on **Bridge Street**, there is the spirit of a crusty old sea captain who delights in attacking a guest or two, then continues to annoy them by tampering with the lights.

***

The Legend of Indian Well began on Ocean Drive in 1745. Jonathan Easton, a wealthy landowner, kept a store of rum which he entrusted to his housekeeper. Refused a drink, a cantankerous Indian girl with a thirst for liquor murdered the housekeeper and threw her lifeless form into the well.

Later, when Easton returned home and found his servant dead, the woman's ghost materialized, accusing the Indian of being her murderer. Three times Easton saw the vision before he finally arranged an investigation. Eventually, the housekeeper's body was found and the Indian girl was arrested and executed.

***

Almost too fantastic is the much-documented tale of a phantom coach and four horses seen galloping up the driveway after midnight at **25 Greenough Place**. While none of the current residents of this 19th century three-story apartment house have beheld the Cinderella-like scene, at least one young woman can attest to a ghostly cat scurrying across a room and a transparent woman wearing turn-of-the-century garb.

***

Before **Prescott Farm** (West Main Road, Middletown) was restored as a colonial museum by Doris Duke's Newport Restoration Foundation, it was the family home of Barbara "Kittymouse" Norman Jones Cook.

Kittymouse was an energetic woman who lived in Prescott House, named for the British general who was captured there by Colonel William Barton in 1777. Since Prescott was seized from the bed of his mistress, it may be his dear lover's ghost who had startled Kittymouse on many occasions. The spirit she described was that of a woman with long, black hair wearing a very pretty water-silk taffeta dress with a small bodice and velvet buttons.

Years later, Kittymouse reported meeting yet another ghost at Prescott Farm, this time the spirit of a Hessian soldier.

***

In order to disprove the legend that there were ghosts living at the old *Astors* mansion (Bellevue and Ruggles avenues), two cynics decided to stay overnight and investigate the home. They saw no spirits during their short stay but they did find angry flames reflected in a mirror. The next day the mansion burned down!

***

Near the *Castle Hill Coast Guard Station* lived Tanya Rhinelander, a woman who never wanted to communicate with the spirit world. Nevertheless, after a particularly troublesome nightmare one evening, she awoke to find the figure of a man wearing colonial garb and a tri-horn hat. Frightened, she turned on the light, but the vision had disappeared.

Tanya speculated that the phantom was most likely John Collins, Rhode Island's governor in the late 1700s, whose body was buried on the Rhinelander property.

Recounting her story to an interviewer, Tanya stated that even if the spook was not the late governor, she was certain she had met a gentleman ghost. How could she tell? "Because he frightened me so much the first time that he never came back!"

***

Fable or not, one of the many stories about *Carey Mansion* (aka Seaview Terrace) is that of a nun who hung herself. Supposedly, the death room is boarded up and every month a priest has to come in and bless the house.

***

There have been several reports that the *Castle Hill Inn & Resort*

Prescott Farm

is haunted. One employee witnessed an apparition (affectionately dubbed Mrs. Agassi) floating down the stairs and through the bar doors of this popular seaside establishment.

***

During one memorable evening, some dinner guests at the old *Grosvenor* mansion (Carroll and Ruggles avenues) lost their appetites after a phantom horseman came galloping up the driveway. They heard the spirit pounding on the door but when the butler went to answer it, there was no one there. But he did hear the horse galloping away!

***

Some nasty ghosts have claimed a carriage house on the usually quiet *Tuckerman Avenue* in Middletown. These malevolent spirits are constantly throwing things and spooking rentors from the premises.

***

If you believe all the rumors, there are more than sugarplums dancing at the *Clement C. Moore House* on Catherine Street.

Although the beloved author of "A Visit From St. Nicholas" was born and raised a New Yorker, Newporters tend to claim Dr. Clement C. Moore as one of their own.

The Moores built their four-story Victorian summer home (then called The Cedars) in Newport and enjoyed an active social life until Dr. Moore died here at age 83 on July 10, 1863.

Some former residents and visitors claim to have seen spooks walking the halls and staircases and spirit children disappearing into solid walls. However, as of this writing, no mortal has caught a glimpse of either the late doctor nor his "right jolly old elf".

***

Sometimes a fable is disproved, yet still perpetuated even after the truth is discovered. Such is the case of *Ochre Court*, the magnificent summer home of New York real estate developer Ogden Goelet, which is now the administration building at Salve

Regina University.

Reportedly, Ochre Court was the haunted domain of a young girl who had fallen to her death from a second story window. But in 1995, one adventurous student discovered that the myth was pure bunk. The girl in question was now a woman—and very much alive, thank you!

***

MANSIONS. Colonials. Beaches. Music festivals. Tennis tournaments. Sailing regattas. Food festivals. These are the images we treasure most about Newport, Rhode Island. The exciting Newport. The historic Newport.

Yet there is another side to this beautiful City-by-the-Sea, one that is rarely found in guidebooks. It is a side that is often strange and incredible and certainly not for the faint-hearted. It has been well-hidden—until now.

So grab your amulets, your incense and your courage. You are about to embark on an armchair tour of real ghost sightings in Newport County, as described by the people who lived to tell them.

Scoff if you must, but know the truth.

Eerie Encounters

S hould you ever have an occasion to walk by a certain farmhouse on Oliphant Lane in Middletown and detect the sweet aroma of piping hot cocoa and freshly baked cookies, consider yourself lucky. You have most likely stumbled upon the happy domicile of Mrs. Murphy, long deceased but not forgotten and still residing at her former home.

For thirty-five years, the kindly Mrs. Murphy has entertained its current owners, first appearing in their children's bedroom in the early 1960s. One late evening, one of the owners was leaving the bathroom when she stopped dead in her tracks. Directly in front of her was the figure of an extremely tall and large woman. They looked at each other for several moments and then the paler of the two disappeared into the air.

Since that time, the spirit has been seen on numerous occasions. "No, we are not afraid to live here," the owner insists. Perhaps it is because her home feels so warm and loving, "like you've been hugged," she says.

Sadly, very little is known about Mrs. Murphy except that she adored the neighborhood children and would bake them cookies and serve hot cocoa on cold, blustery days. Coincidentally, the house is still a magnet for children today.

While the family does not fear the kindly spirit, they are still curious about her life. One answer to the puzzle was solved when an old photo was discovered in the attic. Just one glance at the large woman standing in front of their beloved farmhouse and they knew they had found their cookie lady!

***

This Way Out

There is a house on Division Street that harbors both a male and a female ghost. Although considered friendly, the two are responsible for some interesting occurrences. Lights turn on by themselves, objects explode and feet march up and down the stairs. On one occasion, the owner was reprimanded by the female ghost with a very firm thump on the head!

While the two ghosts share this 1750 colonial, neither may be aware of the other.

Says the owner: "With a house as old as this, it's been through so many machinations in one way or another. So much tumult since Revolutionary days—so many nationalities and people of different ethnic backgrounds have inhabited the homes for one reason or an-other—that you just can't automatically assume that if there is more than one spirit that indeed they are from the same century."

While she doesn't feel any particular malevolence from the ghosts, the owner does think they bid for attention at times.

Still unexplained is the incident of an amethyst vase. Weighing no more than three pounds, the vase had been treasured for thirty-five years until one day it mysteriously burst into tiny fragments. "It sounded as if a bullet had gone through the room and exploded it." Yet there were no bullet holes in any of the windows.

One evening, a houseguest was in the bathroom washing his hands when he happened to look up and see a tiny woman wearing a pretty 18th century blue dress.

"She had these big panels on the side of her dress that stuck out and made her hips look huge."

The guest was not used to such gracious hospitality. The ghost alarmed him so much that he simply unlocked the front door, got into his car and drove directly home!

***

Widow of the Sea

On this eve of gloomy mist, the foghorns moaned steadily in the distance, their resonance clear and comforting. A fleet of groaning vessels swayed in the harbor, illuminated by the glow of the powdered lights ashore. While the good citizens of The Point lay snug and sleeping, the blithe spirit of a sea captain's wife was quite awake, floating in and out of the rooms at Bogart Blakeley's house on Cherry Street.

"Elizabeth was a prankster," Bogart recalled. "She'd move things around. Say you'd put down a coffee cup—and you knew exactly where you put it—and you came back, it was somewhere else."

Once this quaint community of 18th century colonials was the center of much export activity. There were skilled and talented furniture makers like the Townsends and the Goddards, and there were many other folks who produced pewter, candles and clocks. Merchants and craftsmen built their homes in The Point and, since it was so accessible to the water, the area was a logical choice for sea captains, as well.

Perhaps Elizabeth's sea captain never did return home. Yet romantics would surmise that it was her undying love for her husband that kept Elizabeth earthbound.

After ripping down a wall one day, Bogart and his mother, Mrs. G. Bogart Blakeley, discovered an old letter from a friend who was worried that she had not heard from Elizabeth.

"I think she wanted to desperately reply to her friend," mused Mrs. Blakeley, a devout ghost believer from England. Alas, poor Elizabeth never got the chance to respond, for she died of pneumonia a few days later.

At night, the spirit of Elizabeth would roam the wooden stairs and guests often heard her footsteps, saw her shadow and felt her chilly, cold breezes. But since Bogart Blakely sold the Cherry Street house, all ghostly disturbances have ceased.

***

Home, Sweet Haunt

Those who are lucky enough to have an old-fashioned hearth in their dining room or kitchen know the warmth and charm it adds to their home. Seems it is also the spot where one family on Elm Street caught a glimpse of their resident ghost.

Built in 1760, the two-story gambrel-roofed house was purchased by its present owners in 1985. The original house had a total of six rooms—three upstairs and three downstairs—which surrounded a center chimney. The house was enlarged in the late 1800s and there are now a total of five fireplaces, including the hearth with the dutch oven in the keeping/dining room, an area large enough for a person to stand up in.

Late one Saturday afternoon in the 1980s, the husband and wife were sitting in their living room when they were startled by a ghostly woman in a grey colonial dress, white apron and bonnet. In a flurry, she ran down the stairs and into the keeping/dining room. Then she began to prepare the evening meal in the fireplace.

"I felt surprised, but very comfortable because it's a warm house," the husband says. "It appeared as if she was getting the meal ready for her family and she just smiled at us. We didn't feel threatened at all, just a nice warm feeling that we were sharing this home with her and her family."

For most folks, it is difficult enough to share their lives with human beings; they don't need a ghost to keep things interesting. But for one very contented family on Elm Street, they are happily haunted—and loving it.

Newport Waterfront

Spooks in the Stables

The blacksmith heard the singing first, then couldn't believe his eyes. He had worked at **Glen Farm** that night and had not intended to fall asleep in his truck. When his eyes finally adjusted to the dark, he could see the little girl in the swing, her red hair flying. *"If you paint a door today, you will die,"* she sang over and over.

The blacksmith told neighbors that the little red-haired girl was not real at all. She was a ghost. Demonic. Evil. Definitely bad news.

You can't work at Glen Farm too long before you begin to hear the tales. The little red-haired girl. The tall man in the colonial garb and hat. The spook kids.

Most employees begin as skeptics for Glen Farm is considered to be one of Portsmouth's most beautiful and peaceful settings, as frightening as a cottontail rabbit. Not your typical ghost haunt here.

But there is one woman who lived at Glen Farm who will never forget her horrific dealings with a smelly, male ghost. She says he appeared to her at least three times and she was so unnerved by the experiences that she has since moved to another state. The following is her story:

"It was a bit after four a.m. when I rose to get a drink of water from the kitchen. I saw a man crouching on the floor by the refrigerator.

He wore a large hat, a long dark waistcoat and knickers. I could not see his face for his hat brim was covering it, but I did detect some dark hair sticking out.

And then suddenly his head started rolling upward and the noise that emanated from his throat was like a roar from the bowels of hell."

The figure smelled bad, like something decomposing. Checking the locks in the barn apartment, she found them untouched. In the meantime, the ghost had vanished.

On another evening, she was holding onto one of the horses in the wooden barn. Suddenly, the lights went out, which she couldn't understand since she had been standing directly across from the light switch all the time.

"It was right then that I felt that same awful feeling and started smelling that smell again."

Concerned she was going crazy, the woman sought the aid of a spiritualist from Boston. Indeed, he verified that there was at least one troublesome phantom hanging out at Glen Farm—he could hear its demonic laugh. Nevertheless, the man told her not to worry, an idea she found ludicrous. *Don't be afraid?*

"The fear was so uncontrollable. That's like asking somebody not to have their heart beat—or not to breathe."

There have been other ghost encounters at Glen Farm, particularly in a second floor bathroom. While taking a shower, a man felt a hand touch his hair, turned around to grab it and found nothing there.

Then there was the time when a Glen Farm visitor interrupted a young man in a white fisherman's sweater. He apologized and left, then waited a long time before he opened the bathroom door again. Since there was no other way out, the visitor was surprised to find that the man in the sweater had gone.

Glen Farm was first settled in 1638 by Giles Slocum and for the next two hundred years, it remained a collection of small family farms. In the 1800s, New York industrialist Henry A. C. Taylor bought Glen Farm so that he could selectively breed horses for hunting, racing and polo. His son, Moses, fashioned it after a model gentleman's farm with eight hundred acres and, after the death of Reginald Taylor, the farm was sold off. In 1989, it was purchased by the Town of Portsmouth to preserve the open space.

According to legend, Giles Slocum's two children were killed by an Indian slave, who was subsequently hung in Newport. Yet most of the farm's employees believe that it is the ghost of Giles (and at least one of his children) who are making life interesting these days.

Deidre Sharp started working at Glen Farm in 1985. The first time she saw something was a very fleeting glimpse of a child leaving through a door. She didn't think much about it at the time.

"A year later on Easter Sunday, I was at the farm alone and I had taken my horse out. It was really nice and warm and I was giving

him a bath, letting him eat some grass.

All of a sudden he stopped eating and raised his head, looking over at the wooden barn.

The hayloft doors were open, which was strange because they are not opened until the summer. I saw a little red-haired girl walk away from the hayloft door. She was about twelve years old and dressed in a colonial outfit—a dark brown dress with something white in the front, like a petticoat with white lace.

She didn't smile. She had a stern expression on her face. She looked right at us and then she just walked away and blended into the background."

The second incident occurred in 1990, while Deidre was cleaning out stalls in the wooden barn.

"I looked up at the tack room and this man in this weird plantation-like hat and the little red-haired girl floated by the door. I did not hear them walk nor have the sensation of them walking. I did not see their feet."

There is a basement under that particular floor, Deidre explains, so anytime a person walks upon it, their stepsare heard quite distinctly.

Is the man Giles Slocum? Is the little red-haired girl evil? All Deidre knows for certain is that she got a bitterly cold and eerie sensation whenever they appeared.

"They were there to scare me—that was my impression."

***

What the Cat Knew

If there is a ghost lurking about, you can be sure your resident cat or dog will know before you do, the experts say. Such was the case when Jane Berriman brought her cat to spend the night at **Admiral Farragut Inn** (31 Clarke Street).

"Usually, you can take this cat anywhere and do anything with her. But this time, she never stopped screaming the entire time we were there."

When guests check in to this historic 16th century inn, their appetites are whetted for gourmet breakfasts of Stuffed French

Glen Farm

Toast with Sauteed Apples and Apple Cider Syrup. They don't expect to get a ghost with their orange juice.

Former Newport mayor Patrick Kirby, who once owned the building, had a visitor from Ireland awake one night to discover the spirit of a 16th century French soldier.

Years later, after Jane and her husband Bruce had purchased the inn, their sales manager witnessed an apparition going in and out of the basement, the oldest part of the house. The ghosts rarely make an appearance, Jane says, but some people are just spooked by a feeling—and with good reason:

"When we were re-doing the house to make it into an inn, of course we had to have bathrooms. One of our carpenters was painting the new half bath and every time he would go in there his hair on his arms literally stood up. He said, 'I can't go in there anymore.'

It turned out that in the 1950s, a woman had died and was waked in that very room!

***

Goosebumps

One chilly winter's eve in February, a group of writers gathered around a large table in the library, anxious to begin their bi-weekly meeting.

A sparkling chandelier illuminated the room in a warm, antique glow, exposing its delicate, pastel stained glass window, handsome woodwork and elephant skin walls. Next to the fireplace was an overstuffed chair and a small table with two golden bottles of sherry. It was a pleasant room, filled with history and pride, a treasure trove of ship models and leather bound books. It was the type of room that had enticed many a catnap on sun-streamed days.

Jade Hall sat at that same table that night, appearing just a bit nervous, complaining that she was cold. She stared ahead at the elephant skin wallpaper, trying to concentrate on the story one writer was narrating. *It was happening again.* Yet she had no wish to disrupt the meeting with the announcement that a ghost was standing directly behind her.

When the meeting had ended, Jade lingered behind to meet with the owners of the inn, Randy and Selma Fabricant, who invited her to explore their home.

Designed for Hamilton Hoppin by Richard Upjohn in 1853, **The Inn at Shadow Lawn** had been used as a women's club, naval housing, and a bed and breakfast.

Despite its overall tranquility, there had been a few disruptions which the Fabricants wanted Jade to explain. Occasions when lights turned on by themselves, jars fell from shelves and perfume bottles slid across dressers unaided. Occasions when doors opened and closed by themselves or the time an invisible hand tapped a guest on the shoulder. Or when a phantom appeared in one of the guest rooms, transforming its ghoulish coloring from a filmy white to a veiled black.

The Fabricants had learned of Jade's psychic abilities and were anxious to learn the truth. *Was there a ghost at Shadow Lawn?*

Careful not to mention the specter she had seen in the library, Jade assured the owners that if there were entities in their home, they had no evil inclinations.

They followed her through the rooms and up and down the staircases, hoping Jade would prove their suspicions correct. When they reached the basement catacombs, Jade shivered, refusing to enter one of the grey-bricked rooms.

"There is much sorrow here...sickness." That is when the Fabricants told Jade about rumors of a tunnel in the basement, a possible extension of the Underground Railroad.

By the end of her visit, Jade would divulge very little except that there were definite presences. She preferred not to identify them at that point because the Fabricants had to live there and she did not wish to frighten them. Understandably, the Fabricants found this news rather disappointing, but thanked her for her time.

That night, as she stepped outside and into her waiting cab, Jade wondered if she had made a mistake by not telling the Fabricants everything she knew.

Would they have been able to sleep, she wondered, knowing that a tall, lanky, distinguished-looking "man" with peppery hair and a grey suit had watched and followed them from the library and up the staircase?

Gilded Ghouls

Darkness. It is late October and the dead leaves swirl fast around their feet as the guests make their way across the gravel and onto the grass until they are standing at the doorway of destiny. One by one they enter the great neon mouth. The black-bearded pirate. The red vinyl Santa. The green wicked witch.

The gathering is a special one for by midnight, two hundred costumed mortals will have disappeared into the secret tunnel, the air thick with dust. They giggle and feel their way through the glowing maze of sticky cobwebs, bony skeletons and man-eating arachnids, twisting left and right and up a flight of stoney slabs until they find themselves right in the middle of Belcourt Castle's glitzy, glittery medieval banquet hall, and what may be the best Halloween party in Newport.

Dancing and devouring a lavish buffet is a strange smorgasbord of party guests. Some glitter and shine like royalty, while others appear as walking deformities; their bodies purposely maimed and their sick tongues waving suggestively through slots of rubber flesh. Truly, the castle couldn't be a more appropriate setting for a monster mash, since Belcourt claims nearly a dozen ghosts on its spirited roster.

Designed to emulate Louis XIII's hunting lodge at Versailles, Belcourt was built for Oliver Hazard Perry Belmont in 1894 by famed architect Richard Morris Hunt. During The Gilded Age, Belcourt played host to hundreds of galas, and in 1955 and 1956, was the site of Newport's first jazz festival.

The Tinney family (Harold, Ruth, son Donald and Nellie Fuller, Ruth's aunt and guardian) bought the 60-room mansion in 1956 and dubbed it "Belcourt Castle." As art restorers and antiques lovers, the Tinneys had found the perfect home for their expanding art collection, and on July 28, 1957, the doors opened to the public for the first guided tours of the internationally-recognized museum.

In the late 1970s, "Demon Murders" (a movie starring Andy Griffith and Eddie Albert) was filmed at Belcourt Castle. "They shot all the exorcism scenes here for two days," recalls Mrs. Donald (Harle) Tinney. "There was a ghost expert with the crew who told us there were definitely spirits here."

This news was hardly surprising to the Tinneys for family members and guests had reported seeing several spirits over the years. One night, Ruth Tinney awoke to discover a ghost in an 18th century military uniform throwing clothes on top of her bed. Another phantom, The White Lady (thought to be Mrs. Caroline Belmont, Oliver's mother), may have been responsible for throwing a woman out of a chair.

Photographer Keith Henry had joined a Belcourt Castle ghost tour one day when he witnessed the incident in the upstairs French Gothic Ballroom.

"Virginia was introducing this particular chair that was supposed to be haunted by The White Lady. What you were allowed to do was to hold your hand above the chair and when you lowered your hand and if the ghost was present you could possibly feel a tingling in the hand.

This elderly woman sat down in the chair and it took about one second and wham—off the chair! Everyone was astounded and I asked if she would mind doing that again so I could get a picture for the newspaper.

Again, the woman sat in the chair and again she was thrown from it. "Her hands appeared to be two or three inches off the arm of the chair," Keith recalls. "Her feet were straight out in front of her and her bottom was off the chair about two or three inches."

The White Lady isn't the only specter to haunt the ballroom. Harle Tinney had experienced a bit of medieval mayhem there herself, this time from a suit of armor:

"No one was home so I thought it was strange that the lights were on in the ballroom. Being naturally conservative and not wanting to burn the electricity unnecessarily, I went through the ballroom to turn out the lights. After I had turned off the switch, there was very little light left.

As I passed the front of the armor, something screamed at me. It was a horrible and loud, roaring sound.

Then the lights went back on and I turned them off again and the armor screamed. When it screamed a third time, I ran as fast as I could from the room. The scream was terrifying. It sounded like someone was being killed."

Harle had met her first ghost in 1961. "I woke up and saw a man standing beside the bed. My first thought was that he was an intruder. He had on a long, brown robe and a hat that covered his face or head."

Frightened, she nudged Donald, who calmly told her to go back to sleep. Instead, Harle watched the figure in the robe walk right through the wall and disappear.

The next day, Harle learned that her new family was well-acquainted with the monk, a mysterious phantom whom they met initially in the doorway of "Seaverge", the Tinneys' first home in Newport. The family believed the ghost was associated with their acquisition of a statue of a German monk (circa 1600). When the family moved to Belcourt in 1956, the monk statue was placed on a 15th century Italian cassone in the Grand Hall on the first floor.

September 1971 marked the first time that Belcourt Castle would be open for evening tours with dinner. During one particularly busy tour day, Harold Tinney was ascending the Grand Staircase when he spied what appeared to be a floating arm pointing to the Renaissance painting of Mary Magdalene. The next morning, as the second tour of the day ascended the Grand Staircase, the painting fell, barely missing the visitors and smashing its 17th century frame to bits.

The Tinneys believe that the floating arm belonged to the monk who tried to forewarn them of the accident.

Psychics who have visited Belcourt have intimated that the monk is not a good spirit. Yet he was a friend to Ruth Tinney. After her hospitalization in 1993, she returned to Belcourt, where the monk came into her bedroom and "just looked and looked at me." Mrs. Tinney died in December 1995, but before her death she told family members that the monk had returned to her side during three occasions.

With so many phantoms running about, Belcourt Castle is frequently in the news, and the Tinneys are often accused of exploiting their ghosts.

Harle Tinney pooh-poohs these critics. "If ghosts are going to live at Belcourt Castle, they might as well earn their living!"

***

Ghosts on Campus

The assignment was to investigate the many so-called hauntings reported on campus. The participants were a group of students at Salve Regina University. The project sounded fairly simple and maybe even fun. After all, who doesn't like to talk about ghosts?

Belcourt Castle

Not the campus security office, as one disappointed student soon discovered. No one there would verify the rumors that an officer had seen "Bloody Mary," the floating woman at **Ochre Court** whose bloody wrists were bound with chains.

Another student had better luck finding witnesses to talk about the strange occurrences at **Watts-Sherman House**, the 17th century Queen Anne Tudor on Shepard Avenue. In Room 200, residents reported that the clock radio would turn on and off by itself.

Meanwhile, their neighbors in Room 203 would swear their television had a mind of its own, turning off automatically as if it knew when the students had finished watching for the evening. But as annoying as these episodes were, they proved tame when compared to what one young eyewitness beheld, an incident which never was explained:

"One night, the desk worker started to scream. So we all ran downstairs. She said there was a face in the monitor. We didn't believe her at first, but then we saw it for ourselves.

It was a lady sitting on a chair and she looked like she was talking on a telephone. Her image was outlined— darker than the rest of the screen—like a photographic negative."

As the "Collinwood" backdrop of the old "Dark Shadows" television series (starring Jonathan Frid and Alexandra Moltke (aka Alexandra Isles), Claus von Bulow's former mistress), it is intriguing that **Carey Mansion** would have assembled its own cast of spooks and poltergeists, although vampires have yet to make their blood-thirsty appearance.

Today, the Ruggles Avenue mansion is a Salve Regina dormitory where smoke detectors go off for no reason, bottles fly off desks, and radios turn on and off by themselves. One student remembers being warned by his new roommate that there were ghosts at Carey Mansion. He didn't think much of it until he saw something unexplainable.

"My room was completely dark. The window shades were closed. Then this white light showed up on the wall from nowhere. It freaked

us out, but nothing bad happened."

Reports of cold, ghostly presences and an invisible dinner party run amok at **Wakehurst**, the former Ochre Point Avenue home of railroad heir James Van Alen. People have walked by and looked up to see a man's face peering out at them from the attic window. He is dressed in old-fashioned equestrian gear and is also suspected of lurking around the staircase.

Salve ghostsighters also won't want to miss the first snowfall at Wakehurst, when one might get a peek at yet another deceased dweller there—a woman pushing an old baby carriage.

Nearly Departed

Twelve large trucks pulled away from the raven black mansion, their heavy load a treasure to no one but the deceased owner herself, a Victorian spinster whose penchant for art and drama were well-known.

For this last scenario, the Atlantic Ocean provided a hypnotic, almost sensual backdrop the woman would have surprisingly approved of—its salty tongue lapping at the shore, stroking and teasing. Indeed, she had spent many a summer day on the Cliff Walk, gazing out at the grey-green ocean, so near to her dear Arcadia.

She had watched the gulls, admiring their wings of gliding silver as they divebombed into the foam. Standing there with the wind on her cheeks, she had dared to dream and ponder the sorrows of her lonely and troubled existence.

But now that stage had darkened, the last breath resigned. It was 1948 and Beatrice Turner was dead and her house emptied. Soon, the trucks would unload their cargo to an angry blaze, a woman's lifetime of self portraits and diaries lost forever among the ashes.

As a little girl, Mary Samuels would watch the beautiful Beatrice and her mother, Adele, as they strolled past her house on their way to the art association.

"It was during the Flapper days, when everyone was in the short skirts and high-heeled shoes, but Beatrice and her mother still wore the clothes of the Colonial Dames—long dresses right down to their ankles, long white gloves and great big picture hats. And they both carried parasols so they wouldn't get sun on their beautiful white skin."

Beatrice was the only child of Adele and Andrew Turner, a cotton merchant from Philadelphia who bought Arcadia (now **Cliffside Inn**) as a summer retreat in 1907. Although very sweet-natured, poor Beatrice didn't appear to have any real friends, but seemed totally devoted to her parents.

Unlike her beautiful daughter, Adele was not particularly attractive and could be downright domineering, insisting that Beatrice be available to her always. Andrew, on the other hand, had formed a different kind of attachment, discouraging suitors from his daughter's door while professing an unhealthy love for her in his rhythmical dedications:

> *When looking at thy form divine*
> *Perfect in each curve and line*
> *And gazing at thy silken hair*
> *And basking in thy orbits rare*
> *A misnomer 'twas in naming thee*
> *Aught else but Venus*

A talented child, Beatrice yearned to paint and was a student at Pennsylvania Academy of Fine Arts before Andrew discovered she was painting nude models. He demanded she quit and encouraged her to concentrate on painting her own image instead. Beatrice happily complied, producing thousands of self portraits for her father's approval.

Some say Beatrice went mad when Andrew died in 1913. So intent was she to paint her father's portrait that she propped up his decaying body and refused to let it be taken away until she was finished days later. Was it her way of showing love for her father? Or had she finally obtained control?

As if all this weren't fuel enough for the gossips, Beatrice ordered the house to be painted a funereal black. "We were scared to death running by that house," Mary Samuels recalls. "We called it 'The Haunted House'."

Built in 1880 by Governor Thomas Swann of Maryland and used as a private school and nursing home, today's Cliffside Inn is hailed for its grandeur and comfort as a four-star bed and breakfast. Vibrantly colored in plum, rose and coral, there are skylights over grand, ornate beds, fluffy pillows and fireplaces in each guest room.

Most noticeable is the tribute to Beatrice Turner herself, whose lovely face adorns the walls of the entire house, now owned by former television executive Winthrop Baker.

While setting the tables for breakfast in the main parlor, a former innkeeper thought he saw a figure of a woman in a dark blue, full length dress with a high collar. She had her hands on her hips and when he turned again to look, she was gone.

"Some men have come up to me and said they can feel her presence throughout the whole house," former assistant manager Laura LaDuke says. "One said that he kept getting woke up several times during the night and there was a lady standing at the end of his bed."

Beatrice Turner never did marry and continued to wear her outdated apparel (even while mowing the lawn) until she died of cancer at age 59.

Today, the good and dutiful daughter with the beautiful smile and sad, haunting eyes remains a fixture at Cliffside Inn, returning every summer to her beloved Arcadia. From its sun-splashed foyer, it is not so difficult to envision the lovely Beatrice in her long, Victorian dress, sweeping ever so lightly against the steps as she descends the staircase.

"All of my life I have done just what my family wished me," Beatrice wrote in her diary. "I am leading a life I did not choose."

***

The Party's Over

One thing everybody says about **Vernon House** is that it loves a party.

Located at the corner of Clark and Mary Streets, this 18th century home owned by Margaretta Clulow is warm and inviting and, as the French headquarters during the Revolutionary War, entertained such prominent guests as Lafayette and George Washington.

It was during one of her many dinner parties that Margaretta noticed an uninvited guest. The man wore simple, dark blue 18th century dress and was walking past the door and up the stairs. Since no one else was in costume that evening, Margaretta supposed she had seen a ghost. Indeed, it was even possible he was the long-deceased Metcalf Bowler, once a Chief Justice of the Rhode Island Supreme Court and former owner of the house.

"The man who bought this house in 1759, Metcalf Bowler, was quite disreputable. They found out in 1931 that he was a double agent for the British. He got away with it and no one ever knew this until these letters were found in a university out west where they had been sent.

He was a very crooked politician and he built this house for show."

Vernon House also played host to another strange incident. Margaretta continues:

"I knew of a man who came here to a party as a guest and he

Vernon House

entered into a great deal of political talk about Rhode Island and Newport.

After the other guests had left, I went upstairs to turn out the lights. As I was coming down the stairs, he was standing on the landing and he looked up at me and said, 'I don't know what the matter is, but it's very bad right here on the landing.'"

The man complained of being cold and it was then that Margaretta began taking his statement more serious, since "the chill is one of the dead giveaways" of spectral activity. She says he was still feeling uncomfortable when he escaped to his car and drove away.

Oddly enough, that same man turned out to be "a very bad egg" and Margaretta found it interesting that her house did not want him around.

Could it be that Metcalf Bowler was expressing his displeasure?

Or perhaps Judge Bowler was merely conveying—as long as he had to hang around anyway—that there could be only room for one crooked politician at Vernon House!

***

Boogeyman in the buff

Well known for its hospitality, **Hydrangea House** is an alluring inn of European elegance, a former music school located directly across from the Hotel Viking at 16 Bellevue Avenue. It was built in 1876 and, by all accounts, has never had any incidents which would have created "bad vibes."

But there was one very unfortunate couple who experienced bad vibes—and perhaps a bit more.

When you're in the hospitality business, your first priority is your guests. So when a couple complained of feeling "a very strong spirit" in the reading room, co-owners Dennis Blair and Grant Edmondson investigated immediately.

They found nothing and Dennis remembers that the couple were quite shaken. As if this were not sufficient enough to frighten them, the couple had identical nightmares that night, the nature of which they refused to divulge.

A cozy lair of navy blue walls, wing-backed chairs and hydrangea wreaths, the reading room is also where an English writer from Bermuda reported seeing a naked man.

Apparently the man was invisible for again Dennis and Grant investigated and again they found nothing. Still, the woman insisted she was not suffering delusions. Certainly, she knew a naked man when she saw one!

Neither hide nor hair has been seen of the intruder since, leaving Dennis and Grant to conclude that their beloved Hydrangea House was just a onetime romp for a ghost in the buff!

***

Table for one

It was late afternoon and inside the **White Horse Tavern**, Rafael Medina led the way up the narrow, creaking stairs to the second floor dining room where he swore he saw it.

The wall lanterns were lit, casting a warm, amber glow along the walls and wooden beams of the 17th century tavern. The dining tables were set for dinner, and as he passed the upstairs bar, Rafael grew more excited, more animated.

"The table" was in The Pub Room, next to one of the wall-length fireplaces. Rafael pointed out the exact place he was standing when he discovered the stranger, then plopped himself down in "the chair".

"It was my first winter here and it was slow, with only a couple of customers downstairs. I came upstairs for a bottle of wine."

The stranger was a middle-aged man, possibly in his fifties.

"He was dressed in what appeared to be old-time traveling clothes and he had a hat in his hand and looked distracted— he wasn't looking my way. It all happened very fast and when I turned around, there was no one there."

Once owned by the notorious pirate William Mayes, today's White Horse Tavern is a landmark, believed to be the oldest tavern in the United States. Situated on the corner of Farewell and Marlborough Streets, the colonial red building is known more for its exquisite cuisine and historical setting, than its occasional ghost.

On one evening, Rafael and a co-worker were closing down for the night when they heard loud footsteps overhead.

"The floors are two planks deep. You can hear anybody who walks upstairs, even if they're wearing sneakers."

Knowing that all the customers and employees had left long ago, they each grabbed a weapon and with a peppermill clutched firmly in his hand, Rafael searched the entire building. He found no sign of trespassers and, as suspected, all the doors and windows were locked.

Was it really a ghost? Rafael says yes and was so intrigued, he did some research at the Newport Historical Society to learn more. He discovered that a traveler had died in the tavern some centuries before.

"And the next day, his traveling companion stole all of his things and disappeared."

Was the traveler murdered? Did the victim return to the tavern in spirit, expecting to be served a satisfying meal of Beef Wellington or Chateaubriand? While Rafael doesn't have the answers, he does suspect the ghost still haunts White Horse Tavern.

"I truly believe that there are ghosts. There's just so much about the universe that we don't know."

White Horse Tavern

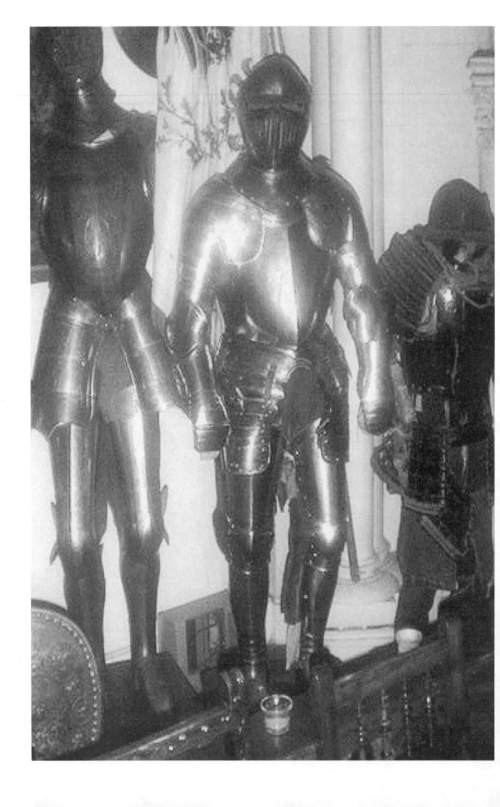

A Ghost Stalkers Guide

From T. F. Green Airport (Warwick, Rhode Island): 25 miles to Newport.
From Boston Logan Airport (Massachusetts): 75 miles to Newport.
From Amtrak (Kingston, Rhode Island): 25 miles to Newport.

Getting Around by Car

(The following routes begin at the Newport County Convention and Visitors Bureau parking lot at 23 America's Cup Avenue:)

America's Cup Avenue: Turn right out of the parking lot. At the traffic light take a right onto America's Cup Avenue heading south toward downtown Newport.

Newport Mansions: Turn left at the first traffic light on America's Cup Avenue onto Marlborough Street which runs between the baseball park and the fire station. Take a right at the first stop sign onto Thames Street, then a left at the traffic light onto Touro Street. On your left will be Eisenhower Park and movie theaters on the right. Touro Street ends at the first traffic light after the Touro Synagogue. Bearing right at the light begins Bellevue Avenue, which leads past the Newport Art Museum on the left and the Old Stone Mill on the right. Proceed through the next traffic light (intersection of Memorial Boulevard and Bellevue Avenue) and the Tennis Hall of Fame is on the left with the Bellevue Shopping Center on the right. Follow directions for the Tennis Hall of Fame, which is located on Bellevue Avenue. Almost all of the mansions are found on this avenue. The Breakers Mansion can be reached by taking a left off Bellevue Avenue onto Ruggles Avenue, the fifth street after the traffic light at the intersection of Bellevue Avenue and Narragansett Avenue. Continuing on Bellevue Avenue leads to scenic Ocean Drive.

Ocean Drive: In the right-hand lane, follow America's Cup Avenue toward downtown to the traffic light at the intersection of America's Cup Avenue and Thames Street (just after the statue of the wave on the right). Turn right onto Thames Street and then bear right onto Wellington Avenue (just across from a Shell gas station on the left-hand side). Continue on to Ocean Drive by taking a right at both of the next two stop signs. Ocean Drive runs past Fort Adams State Park, Hammersmith Farm, Castle Hill Inn & Resort, Brenton Point State Park, Gooseberry, Hazard, and Bailey's Beaches, and ends on Bellevue Avenue, which leads to the mansions, The Tennis Hall of Fame and the downtown area.

The Cliff Walk: Continue south on America's Cup Avenue toward downtown. Stay in the left-hand lane and continue through the intersection of America's Cup Avenue and Thames Street where the road becomes Memorial Boulevard (just after the statue of the wave). Travel up Memorial Boulevard through two traffic lights and across Bellevue Avenue. The entrance to the Cliff Walk is on the right just behind the Cliff Walk Manor. Easton's Beach (First Beach) is on the right after the entrance to the Cliff Walk.

Cemeteries

Arnold Family lot - Pelham St.
Braman Cemetery - Farewell St.
Catholic - Mount Vernon St.
Catholic - Warner St.
Clarke Ground - Dr. Marcus F. Wheatland Blvd.
Clifton Burying Ground - Golden Hill
Coddington Burial Ground - Farewell and North Baptist St.
Coggeshall Family Lot - Coggeshall St.
Collins Cemetery - Castle Hill
Common Burying Ground - Farewell St.
Easton Family Lot - off Annandale Road adjacent to Friends
Island Cemetery - Warner St.
Island Cemetery Annex - Van Zandt
Jewish Cemetery - at intersection Kay St. and Bellevue Ave.
North Burial Ground - Farewell St.
Quaker Ground - Edward St.
Trinity Churchyard - off Spring St.

Events

Haunted Newport Week: A week-long celebration of the darker side of Newport, Rhode Island. For schedule, call Newport County Convention and Visitors Bureau at (800) 976-5122 or see their website at www.GoNewport.com.

Haunted Dining

La Petite Auberge: 19 Charles Street, Newport, RI 02840. Phone: (401) 849-6669.

White Horse Tavern: 26 Marlborough Street, Newport, RI 02840. Phone: (401) 849-3600. Website: www.whitehorsetavern.com

Haunted Lodging

Admiral Farragut Inn: 31 Clarke Street, Newport, RI 02840-3023. Phone: (800) 343-2863. Website: www.admiralsinns.com

Cliffside Inn: 32 Seaview Avenue, Newport, RI 02840. Phone: (401) 847-1811. Website: www.cliffsideinn.com

Hydrangea House: 16 Bellevue Avenue, Newport, RI 02840. Phone: (800) 945-4667. Website: www.hydrangeahouse.com

The Inn at Shadow Lawn: 120 Miantonomi Avenue, Middletown, RI 02842. Phone: (800) 352-3750. Website: www.shadowlawn.com

Organizations

American Society for Psychical Research: 5 West 73rd St., New York, NY 10023. Website: www.aspr.com

Ghost Research Society: P. O. Box 205, Oak Lawn, IL 60454-0205. Website: www.ghostresearch.org

Inernational Ghost Hunters Society: Crooked River Ranch, OR 97760. Website: www.ghostweb.com

New England Society for Psychic Research: P. O. Box 41, Monroe, CT 06468. Website: www.warrens.net

Paranormal Playgrounds

Belcourt Castle: 657 Bellevue Avenue, Newport, RI 02840. Phone: (401) 846-0669. Website: www.belcourt.com

Glen Farm: 163 Glen Farm Road, Portsmouth, RI 02871. Phone: (401) 846-0200. Website: www3.edgenet.net/gfpp

Prescott Farm: 2009 West Main Road, Middletown, RI 02842. Phone: (401) 847-6230.

Periodicals

The Anomalist: P. O. Box 12434, San Antonio, TX 78212. Website: www.anomalist.com

Strange Magazine: P. O. Box 2246, Rockville, MD 20847. Website: www.strangemag.com

Tourism Information

Newport County Chamber of Commerce: 45 Valley Rd., Newport, RI 02842. Phone: (401) 847-1600. Website: www.newportchamber.com

Newport County Convention and Visitors Bureau: 23 America's Cup Avenue, Newport, RI 02840. Phone: (401) 849-8048. Website: www.GoNewport.com

Websites

Dark Side of the Net: www.darklinks.com
The Ghost Watcher: www.flyvision.org/sitelite/Houston/ GhostWatcher/index.html
Invisible Ink: www.invink.com
Obiwan's UFO-Free Paranormal Page: www.ghosts.org
The Shadowlands: www.theshadowlands.net
The Spirit Website: www.ghosthunter.org

GLOSSARY

Amulet - A charm worn in order to bring luck or ward off evil.

Apparition - A ghostly figure or specter.

Clairvoyant - A person who has the power to perceive things that are out of the natural range of human senses.

Doppleganger - A ghost or spirit of a living person.

Earthbound Spirit - A spirit that has not crossed over yet. Usually due to a sudden or tragic death.

Exorcism - The process of expelling evil spirits from an object, person, or place.

Ghost - The spirit of a dead person, especialy one believed to appear in bodily likeness to living persons or to haunt former habitats.

Haunt - A place that is inhabited or visited by a ghost or other supernatural being.

Materialization - The appearance of dead spirits in material form.

Medium - A person thought to have the power to communicate with the spirits of the dead or with agents of another world or dimension.

Ouija board - A divination tool which spells out words or sentences, supposedly conveying messages from the spirit world.

Parapsychology - The study of Psychic Phenomena that can not be explained by natural laws.

Poltergeist - A ghost that manifests itself by noises, rappings, and the creation of disorder.

Possessed - A living person whose personality has been taken over by an evil entity.

Psychic - A person capable of extraordinary mental processes, such as extrasensory perception and mental telepathy.

Psychic Photography - Supernatural or preternatural images appearing on photographic film.

Seance - When a group of two or more people join together for a sitting with intentions of communicating with a spirit. Usually through a medium.

Supernatural - Of or relating to existence outside the natural world, which seems to violate natural forces.

BIBLIOGRAPHY

Bart, Sheldon. "Portraits of the Artist." Country Inns, March/April 1993.

Cunningham, Scott and **Harrington, David.** *The Magical Household.* St. Paul, MN: Llewellyn Publications, 1987,

Davis, Paul. "East Bay Area Boasts Its Share of Ghosts, Murders and Odd Occurrences." Providence Journal-Bulletin, October 30, 1986.

Douglas, James Thomson. "The Faces on the Fence Posts." The Green Light, April 1979.

Federal Writers' Project. *Rhode Island: A Guide to the Smallest State.* Boston, MA: Houghton Mifflin Co., 1937.

Gannon, Thomas. *Newport, Rhode Island: A Guide to the City by the Sea.* Woodstock, VT: The Countryman Press, 1992.

Gavan, Terrence. *Exploring Newport.* Newport, RI: Pineapple Publications, 1992.

The Grist Mill. Newport Daily News, January 15, 1954; April 23, 1954.

Holzer, Hans. *Ghosts, Hauntings and Possessions.* St. Paul, MN: Llewellyn Publications, 1990.

Linn, Denise. *Sacred Space.* New York, NY: Ballantine Books, 1996.

Smith, Martha. "Spooks! Gadzooks!" ProvidenceJournal-Bulletin, October 28, 1985.

Smith, Susy. *Haunted Houses for the Millions.* Bell, 1967.

INDEX

To order additional copies of *HAUNTED Newport* at $10.95 each plus $1.50 postage and handling, please complete and send the order form below:

Order Form

Name _____

Street Address _____

City _____

State _____ Zip _____

Daytime phone _____

<u>Quantity</u>   <u>Price</u>   <u>Total</u>

_____   _____   _____

                add shipping $1.50   _____

                add 7% sales tax   _____

                        TOTAL $ _____

Make checks payable to:
  austen sharp
  P.O. Box 12
  Newport, RI 02840